SPILLED MILK

HAIKU DESTINIES

ALSO BY GARY HOTHAM

BOOK:

Breath Marks: Haiku to Read in the Dark (1999)

CHAPBOOKS:

Without the Mountains (1976)
The Fern's Underside (1977)
Off and On Rain (1978)
Against the Linoleum (1979)
This Space Blank (1984)
Pulling Out the Bent Nail (1988)
As Far As the Light Goes (1990)
The Wind's View (1993)
Before All the Leaves are Gone (1996)
Hair's & Hawk Circles (1996)
Bare Feet (1998)
Footprints & Fingerprints (1999)
The Sky Stays Behind (2000)
Odor of Rain (2004)
Missed Appointment: The Haiku Art (2007)
Sand Over Sand (2009)

Spilled Milk

Haiku Destinies

Gary Hotham

Paintings by Susan Elliott

PINYON PUBLISHING

Montrose, Colorado

Cover art and interior paintings copyright © 2010 by
Susan E. Elliott

Photograph of Gary Hotham copyright © 2010 by
Kimberly Hotham Hamrick

First Edition: 2010

Pinyon Publishing
23847 V66 Trail, Montrose, CO 81403
www.pinyon-publishing.com

Library of Congress Control Number: 2010929334
ISBN: 978-0-9821561-5-5

Acknowledgments

Some of the poems in this book have previously appeared in the following magazines/journals/anthologies:

Acorn
ASHIYA Haiku Festa Anthology (Japan)
Blithe Spirit (England)
bottle rockets
Concise Delight
FrogPond
Haiku Canada Review
The Heron's Nest
HQ (England)
Lilliput Review
Mainichi Daily News Haiku Contests (Japan)
Modern Haiku
Noon (Japan)
Now Culture
Paper Wasp (Australia)
Presence (England)
Puckerbrush Review
Quadrant (Australia)
Roadrunner
Shearsman (England)
Solitary Plover
Vancouver Cherry Blossom Festival Sakura award
White Lotus

Dedication

Mom—

Who cleaned up lots of literal spilled milk
before the crying lasted very long.

Larry & Jan Johnson—

Friends, who we have seen over the many
years, help those who have more to cry over
than just spilled milk.

God Bless You, Mrs. Maloney, Wherever You Are

It has been over 40 years since my first contact with the haiku as a high school sophomore in Mrs. Maloney's English class. Our textbook focused on literature around the world and included a short section on the Japanese haiku. I particularly remember a haiku by Kusatao Nakamura on the greening of spring and his child teething. The image and the moment stuck and has resonated in my memory. I don't remember who did the translation for the textbook but here is R.H. Blyth's version:

Among the myriad leaves of spring
My child has begun
To cut his teeth.

At that time, Mrs. Maloney decided we would write two haiku for homework that she would read aloud in class the next day without attribution. One haiku was to follow exactly the 5-7-5 syllable count while the other could be less strict in form. One might think this an easy assignment but back then writing poetry was not the kind of homework I looked forward to. I don't recall any specifics about the two I wrote other than they attempted to be humorous. I hope the written record of them has vanished into the thin air of such juvenilia. Since then I have written enough bad haiku that have been published and confront me from time to time that I don't need those two coming back to haunt me. But they were my introduction to haiku.

I didn't start writing haiku then, but when I began writing poetry within the next year or so it was a poetic form among the many I attempted from time to time. It was also one I thought I had some success with. When I did start submitting poems to magazines the haiku were the ones that were accepted more than any other type of poem I wrote.

Some time by the end of my first year of university I stopped writing altogether since the frustration became too high between what I wanted for my poetry and what I was producing. And besides, I had too many other interests. But during my last year at university, the urge to write reasserted itself, and the focus of that effort became again the haiku. Its brevity, the sharpness of its imagery, and its penetrating focus on a state of being or a moment in time helped me create the poetry I wanted to write. It is a form that gives me, as James Tipton stated so well, "the possibility of discovering new energy through words put together with precision and emotion." Since then, writing poetry has been a very regular practice for me, and the haiku has been the structure for those poems. So I thank you, Mrs. Barbara Maloney, for what you brought into my life those many years ago. God bless you wherever you are.

—Gary Hotham

Kusatao Nakamura's haiku is found in R.H. Blyth's A History of Haiku, Vol Two, Hokuseido Press, 1964, Tokyo, p. 218.

James Tipton quote from The Haiku Anthology: English Language Haiku by Contemporary American and Canadian Poets, Cor van den Heuvel, editor, Anchor Press/ Doubleday, 1974, New York, p. 270.

A version of this essay first appeared in *Woodnotes*, Issue 31, 1996, edited by Michael Dylan Welch, Foster City, California.

birthday sunrise—
no extra waves
on the ocean

mist lifting off the lake—
children skipping stones
into deeper water

overcast morning—
goldfish touch
the surface

enough sunrise—
a small window
in an old hotel

the day starts
with warnings of snow—
her pile of old birthday cards in the trash

morning walk—
nothing for the stone fence
to stop

among the morning blossoms—
the stone turtle
more stone

turning back on a dead end street—
one odor changes
another

my brother's birthday—
places on the path the rain
can't move out of

dark clouds without warning—
a piece of string not tied
to anything

new plans for the day—
water running away
from the rain

spilled milk—
nothing more
pours out

steady morning wind—
lottery tickets on top
of the trash

my address on the envelope—
a long ago hero
on the postage stamp

street of rain—
the list of errands folded
smaller

at the bus stop—
her hand out
in the rain

wet sand wet feet
what's left
of the wave

more footsteps—
the broken branch
breaks again

mid afternoon break—
eating around the bruise
on the apple

crumbs around my coffee—
no one going by
stops going by

the rest of the day—
cherry blossoms
to spare

a short cut
around parked cars—
afternoon drizzle

express bus—
vacant seats next to
strangers

a big sky bigger—
nothing to catch
my breath

off season ocean—
the dog runs back
to another voice

far away—
carnival lights
changing colors

watching the ocean—
gum wrappers balled up
in my hand

not here long—
a child asks to see
a star fall

a cage
without movement—
early at the zoo

slow squeak—
the cage door
hinges

behind our backs—
the sounds the ocean
covers up

last day—
mountains coming to
an end

dark blues—
the empty halves
of a sea shell

on the phone with an old friend—
shadows with places
to go back to

closing the hotel door—
nothing left behind
ours

her hum—
the shapes never changing back
in the kaleidoscope

scattering fireflies—
stars further away
from their light

scenic stop—
the shadow only a shadow
can touch

drifting into grass—
a child's bubble
the air didn't burst

playground swings—
a strong wind replaces
the children

evening—
no boats on the lake
to come back in

year's end—
eyes inside
a party mask

deep space photos—
nothing but stars
in a starry night

plain darkness—
a firefly blinks with
the speed of light

between stars—
our own thoughts
not as far

thin snowfall—
footprints left
near ours

snow on the ground
snow on my good shoes
for the funeral

bone chilling—
not enough night
for all the stars

new layers of snow—
the rest of the universe
to search on foot

his 44th—
water that doesn't run back
into the ocean

stirring up the sand castle—
a wave all the way
from the ocean

turning over shells—
one new wave
after the other

outside the classroom—
a hallway that goes by
other classrooms

side by side—
children blowing bubbles
that burst in the air

Goethe lived
much of his life near here—
the Buchenwald Memorial

the child's soap bubbles—
a short distance
to out run one

children running from the playground—
leaves left to scatter
by themselves

traffic backs up
from the ambulance—
wild flowers in full bloom

home—
sand rinsed off the shells
with our own water

the sun's warmth—
part of the house
we seldom use

leftover pages
in her photo album—
the room cleaned out

the storm off to one side of the sky—
pieces of her puzzle
that don't fit

the wind not missing our house—
one book missing
from the set

bare floor
around the stain—
an old month on the calendar

protected
by warning signs—
walls left by the Roman Empire

on my way to bed—
what's left of the evening
for the fireflies

weighing down the night—
the empty side
of the bed

too many stars

no one

is near

colder overnight—
the deep water hasn't changed
color

her birthday—
more stars in the puddles
the rain left

before color
before black & white
morning

sunrise warmth

—

the moth's dead
weight

crowded laughs

—

a short breeze carries fewer
cherry blossoms

late summer visitors

—

less morning
for the morning glory

nearly upside down

—

driftwood
in the last wave

noon

—

more rock each time
the ocean moves back

other worlds

—

part of her seashell in some other
hands

high water from the rain

—

his dog soaking up
the river

too heavy
for the river

—

stepping-stones

scenic overlook

—

strangers switching places
with strangers

lingering

—

the top of the ocean
in her hands

mountains
the same distance each day
—

shiny in the rain

wild apples

—

one bite breaks
the skin

cancer survivor
a basket of shells picked off
many beaches

fading daylight

—

the sound as the ocean
runs out

next to the rain
—

window
seats

wind spins

—

half a dozen footprints
the wave didn't spoil

dwindling daylight

—

the last drop nobody
takes

shadows
changing shadows
—

each petal falls like the others

visiting their graves

—

wind scatters plastic flowers
among the real

near sunset

—

children running against
their shadows

worn out day

—

rocks the river left on top
of each other

Saturday night rain
—

each piece of puzzle left
sky

near dark
children begin the game

—

too many places to hide

partly visible moon

—

the ocean leaves its shine
on the shine

middle of the night stars

—

views that take
almost forever

fireworks celebrating

—

stars beyond the sound
beyond the stars

officially winter

—

gray hairs caught
in the bristles

places
for the ocean to end
—

his birthday no longer a party

Short Word Prejudice

"Haiku are great if you only know a bunch of short words." *

This statement about the haiku form came in an e-mail. For a poet it's always good to have friends around to provide their skeptical thoughts about your chosen forms of expression. So once again life's metaphysical pause: why this and not that? The statement was preceded by a paragraph expressing my friend's concern that "haiku poems never use words that would send people to the dictionary." And in his opinion our great American poet, Poe, caught up in the haiku spirit, would never have used tintinnabulation in "The Bells" but something like "to the sound that little silver bells make so musically wells from the bells, bells, bells, bells ... from the tinkling and the jingling of the bells." His statement about the lack of words in a haiku that would send a reader to the dictionary and his example of Poe's word would make one think it is probably not short words that are his concern but words that are too ordinary, too common, too simple. Perhaps there is in the statement the idea that poetry needs difficult and elegant words to elevate it to a higher level of cultural refinement.

It has never entered my mind that one of my

* Lance Maloney, who is, among many other things, a globalizing thinker, rambunctious storyteller, and name-brand coffee addict, in a personal message to the author, December 3, 2007.

goals, as a writer of haiku, is to send my readers to the dictionary. I don't mind if they do go. I suspect most writers think their audience is fairly literate in our language. We don't sit around wondering if our readers understand the words in our poem. It certainly is not the length of the words, however defined, that is our prime concern but whether the words in the grammatical structure of our poetry create the best poem. Sometimes the simple reversal of two words or flipping the lines of our poem can sharpen and deepen the haiku's meaning for the reader way beyond any change of one word for another or a longer word for a shorter one. We are not averse to changing the words. I do not know of any carefully devised scientific surveys to support this but I doubt many poets think they need to prove to the world that they know more than a bunch of short, common, everyday words and so give much thoughtful energy to proving it by changing a short one for a longer one, the common for the strange, the simple for the complex.

My desire as a poet is to let the reader experience the moment, the state of being that is the focus of the haiku, with as much intensity as is possible. I want words that not only recreate the moment but resonate with the reader, that make the experience reverberate, and—especially since it is a haiku—with only those few words that are necessary. A poet works his words hard. I think the haiku form especially favors short words, common words that build but don't distract from the goal. It is possible that a word that might send a reader to the dictionary is the best one to use or that an unusual and uncommon one like 'tintinnabulation' is most appropriate. On the whole I don't want a distraction from the flow. In the poet's bag of skills and tricks knowing well a bunch of short words that do not send people to a dictionary is a distinct advantage. One must be careful: a reader who goes willingly to the dictionary might never come back to the poem.

Some people in our audience who would like a dollop or two of verbosity in their poems may think haiku writers do not like words since they use so few. I don't think that is the case. The poet recognizes the strength of words and wants to highlight that power with as few as necessary. Yes, just enough to intensify the language of the poem for the reader. One thing the poet is doing with a poem is creating a focus on the power of the word. A poet certainly does not believe that "sticks and stones may break my bones but words can never harm me." I suspect most poets are likely to have a greater fear of the lasting damage poorly chosen words can inflict on the reader. Of all people, we poets, even when we fail, should be committed to words that tell the truth. We seek poetry that clarifies rather than hides the essence of our existence.

I think poets ought to be proud, pleased, and happy that they can make powerful haiku out of a few short words. If the universe is made from many very small things, then why not accept the challenge of creating great poems with "a bunch of short words?"

A version of this essay first appeared in *Modern Haiku*, Volume 39:3, Autumn 2008, edited by Charles Trumbull, Santa Fe, New Mexico.

Made in the USA
Middletown, DE
30 July 2015